GO WEST WITH SETTLERS AND FARMERS

Rachel Stuckey

Crabtree Publishing Company
www.crabtreebooks.com

Crabtree Publishing Company
www.crabtreebooks.com

Author: Rachel Stuckey

Consultant: Professor Patricia Loughlin,
University of Central Oklahoma

Managing Editor: Tim Cooke

Designer: Lynne Lennon

Picture Manager: Sophie Mortimer

Design Manager: Keith Davis

Editorial Director: Lindsey Lowe

Project Coordinator: Kathy Middleton

Editor: Janine Deschenes

Proofreaders: Wendy Scavuzzo and Petrice Custance

Children's Publisher: Anne O'Daly

Production coordinator and Prepress techician: Tammy McGarr

Print coordinator: Katherine Bertie

Production coordinated by Brown Bear Books

Photographs:
Front Cover: **Getty images:** Ann Ronan/Picture Collector main; **Bridgeman Art Library:** Peter Newark American Pictures tr; **Shutterstock:** br.

Interior: **Corbis:** Bettmann 17, John C. H. Grabill 10cr; **Civil War Talk:** 21b; **Dreamstime:** Georgina Evans 10bl; **Library of Congress:** 4, 7, 11, 13b, 14tr, 18br, 19, 24-25t, 26tr, 27, 28r; **NOAA:** George E. Marsh Album 22; **Shutterstock:** 16br, 20, Melissa E. Dockstader 18cl, Mikele Dray 16cl, Emattil 28bl, Everett Historical 6, 13t, 21t, 23l, 24br, Margo Harrison 14bl; **Thinkstock:** Terrance Emerson 29, Global 23tr, istockphoto 12, Daniel rao 5; **TNM Past Perfect:** 24l; **Topfoto:** The Granger Collection 15; **Whitney Gallery of Western Art:** Gift of Mrs Sidney T. Miller 26bl.

All other artwork and maps **Brown Bear Books Ltd**.

Brown Bear Books has made every attempt to contact the copyright holder. If you have any information please contact licensing@brownbearbooks.co.uk

Library and Archives Canada Cataloguing in Publication

Stuckey, Rachel, author
  Go West with settlers and farmers / Rachel Stuckey.

(Go West! travel to the wild frontier)
Includes index.
Issued in print and electronic formats.
ISBN 978-0-7787-2330-1 (bound).--
ISBN 978-0-7787-2347-9 (paperback).--
ISBN 978-1-4271-1736-6 (html)

  1. Frontier and pioneer life--West (U.S.)--Juvenile literature.
2. Pioneers--West (U.S.)--Juvenile literature. 3. Farmers--West
(U.S.)--History--19th century--Juvenile literature. I. Title.

F596.S88 2016   j978'.02   C2015-907974-8
                 C2015-907975-6

Library of Congress Cataloging-in-Publication Data

Names: Stuckey, Rachel, author.
Title: Go West with settlers and farmers / Rachel Stuckey.
Description: New York : Crabtree Publishing, 2016. | Series: Go West! Travel to the wild frontier | Includes index. | Description based on print version record and CIP data provided by publisher; resource not viewed.
Identifiers: LCCN 2016001586 (print) | LCCN 2015049886 (ebook) | ISBN 9781427117366 (electronic HTML) | ISBN 9780778723301 (reinforced library binding : alk. paper) | ISBN 9780778723479 (pbk. : alk. paper)
Subjects: LCSH: Pioneers--West (U.S.)--History--19th century--Juvenile literature. | Frontier and pioneer life--West (U.S.)--Juvenile literature. | West (U.S.)--History--19th century--Juvenile literature.
Classification: LCC F596 (print) | LCC F596 .S923 2016 (ebook) | DDC 978/.02--dc23
LC record available at http://lccn.loc.gov/2016001586

Crabtree Publishing Company
www.crabtreebooks.com   1-800-387-7650

Printed in Canada/022016/IH20151223

Published in Canada
Crabtree Publishing
616 Welland Ave.
St. Catharines, Ontario
L2M 5V6

Published in the United States
Crabtree Publishing
PMB 59051
350 Fifth Avenue, 59th Floor
New York, New York 10118

Published in the United Kingdom
Crabtree Publishing
Maritime House
Basin Road North, Hove
BN41 1WR

Published in Australia
Crabtree Publishing
3 Charles Street
Coburg North
VIC, 3058

CONTENTS

What Are the Prospects?

The American West was a place of opportunity. It promised new settlers land to farm and the freedom to build their own communities.

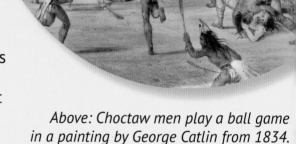

WE WERE HERE FIRST

★ **Native peoples first ...**

... Spanish and Mexicans later

The first inhabitants of the West were Native peoples. For many centuries, the region was home to peoples such as the Apache and Navajo in the south, the Sioux on the plains, the Nez Percé near the Rocky Mountains, and the Haida on Canada's Pacific Coast. Spanish settlers from Mexico arrived in the 1600s in California, the Southwest, and Texas. When settlers came from the East in the early 19th century, they also claimed land that traditionally belonged to Native peoples.

Above: Choctaw men play a ball game in a painting by George Catlin from 1834.

How the West Was Won

★ **Enlarging the United States**

★ **Treaties and war**

Spain, Britain, and France claimed land in the West. American president Thomas Jefferson (left) bought the Louisiana Territory from France in 1803. In 1846, the United States added Oregon in a **treaty** with Britain. Two years later, the United States won the war with Mexico, gaining California, land in the Southwest, and complete control of Texas (1846–1848). The US government encouraged its citizens to move to the new territory, even though parts of it were occupied by Native peoples and Mexicans.

4

Staking a Claim

★ Government offers free land

★ Settlers take advantage

Most settlers were attracted to the West by the promise of land. From early in the 19th century, land could be claimed by anyone prepared to work it. In 1862, the Homestead Act allowed settlers to **stake a claim** to 160 acres (65 hectares) of land. Many farmers headed west in search of better land and new money-making opportunities in the American West. The Canadian government passed the 1872 Dominion Lands Act, making the same promise of land to citizens and **immigrants** settling in the Canadian prairies.

DID YOU KNOW?

Many people came to the West seeking religious freedom. Many settlers were Mennonites from Europe. They wanted to be able to practice their faith freely. The Mormons, an American religious group, also headed west to build their own community in Utah.

To early settlers, the landscape of the Great Plains of the West seemed too harsh to live in.

Just Passing Through

★ The Great Plains ...

not so great for living

The United States acquired the grasslands between the Rocky Mountains and the Mississippi River as part of the Louisiana Purchase. Early settlers thought these Great Plains were **uninhabitable**, with few trees and little water. They passed through them on the way to California and Oregon. Settlers eventually learned that the **prairies** could offer good farming and ranching.

MY WESTERN JOURNAL

Imagine you were thinking about moving to start a new life. Using information on these pages, do you think you would choose the West as your destination?

Meet the Folks

Many different people settled the West. Some included freed black slaves from the South, Mormons, Europeans, Chinese workers, and young Americans seeking fortune and adventure.

MY WESTERN JOURNAL

Imagine you were a former slave from the South. Using information on the previous pages and these pages, do you think you might have moved west?

Give your reasons.

FINDING FREEDOM

★ **Former slaves head west ...**

... then west again ...

Many settlers who headed west were former slaves seeking a chance to make a new life. Some joined the California Gold Rush or worked as cowboys. Many arrived in the late 1870s, after political changes in the South led to them losing many of the freedoms they had gained after slavery ended in 1865. More than 15,000 African Americans moved to the plains of Kansas, but some found the climate there too hard to stay. They returned home or moved farther west. Some moved north, where they settled in the western provinces of Canada. In 1874, for example, African Americans from Dakota Territory moved north to help settle Emerson, the first city in what is now Manitoba.

Traveling West

★ **Travel by ship ...**

... or take a ride

The first American settlers from the East headed to the West by sailing around the bottom of South America. Later adventurers created trails over land. Settlers traveled west by covered wagon in groups called wagon trains. It took six months to cross the continent from the Mississippi River to the Pacific Coast.

EAST MEETS WEST

★ **Chinese workers arrive**

★ **Good habits help survival**

Chinese workers arrived in North America in large numbers after 1848. They came to join the California Gold Rush, or to help build the railroads. They ate a healthy diet of fish, rice, and vegetables, and drank herbal teas. They also bathed daily, which was an uncommon practice, but helped prevent them from getting sick. When the Gold Rush was over and the railroads were built, many Chinese workers settled in Western towns. They found work as cooks or opened businesses, but they often faced prejudice and harrassment.

Right: Chinese miners carry their possessions on poles balanced across their shoulders.

Who Moved Where?

★ **Diversity in the West**

★ **Settlers stick together**

Immigrants from Europe were a large part of the newcomers in the West. These settlers mostly formed communities with people from their own country. They continued to speak their own languages, and kept the traditions of their homelands. Scandinavian settlers went to Minnesota, Germans settled in North Dakota, and Russian Mennonites settled on the Great Plains. Immigrants from these groups also settled in Manitoba, Alberta, and Saskatchewan in Canada.

DID YOU KNOW?

The Mormons were not popular in the eastern United States. In 1847, the Mormon leader Brigham Young led his people west. Over the next 20 years, thousands of Mormons took the Mormon Trail to the Great Salt Lake in Utah.

Fort Edmonton

Fort Edmonton was originally opened by the Hudson's Bay Company as a trading post. The company bought furs from Native American and European trappers to trade with the East.

CANADA

Fort Edmonton

UNITED STATES

Oregon City

Bozeman

Scottsblu

Oregon

The first wagon train set out on the Oregon Trail in 1836. At the time, the trail only stretched partway across the continent. From 1842, however, the trail was extended. In the first few years, about 5,000 people crossed the country to settle in Oregon. In 1846, the United States signed a treaty with Great Britain setting Oregon's borders with Canada.

Sacramento

Salt Lake City

Los Angeles

Santa Fe

Sacramento

Sacramento became an important destination on the California Trail after the discovery of gold at Sutter's Mill there in January 1848.

Salt Lake City

Mormon settlers led by Brigham Young settled Salt Lake City in 1847. They moved to what was then Utah Territory to be able to practice their religion freely.

In the 1800s, settlers from the East headed west on overland trails that crossed the continent.

Key

— Fort Smith–Santa Fe Trail
— Gila Trail
— Mormon Trail
— Santa Fe Trail
— Oregon Trail
— Bozeman Trail
— Old Spanish Trail
— California Trail
— El Camino Real
— Carlton Trail

Fort Garry

Council Bluffs

St. Joseph

Independence

Fort Smith

Independence

The most important departure point for wagon trains heading west was Independence, Missouri. Settlers from the East traveled there by steamboat before setting out on the Oregon Trail, from which other trails branched off.

Locator map

Santa Fe

When the Santa Fe Trail was first opened in the 1820s, Santa Fe was still a Mexican town. Like the rest of the Southwest, it passed to the United States in 1848, after the Mexican–American War.

Let's Get Going

Most settlers traveled west on foot or by wagons pulled by horses or oxen. Between 1836 and 1890, approximately 750,000 people took the wagon trails to the West.

★ ★

Gathering Together

★ **Safety in numbers**

★ **Riding, walking, crawling ...**

Wagon trains began at Independence, Missouri. It was the farthest west people could travel by steamboat. Settlers, traveling along many trails, needed supplies for the journey and for their first winter in the West. The journey across America was 2,200 miles (3,540 km) and took six months. Wagons set out in May so they could make it across the mountains before the snow arrived in the fall.

Above: A settler prepares to set out on the trail with oxen pulling a wagon train.

★ ★

Home Away from Home

★ **Prairie schooners**

★ **Trains on the plains**

Many settlers carried their supplies in large **Conestoga wagons**. The wagons often had hooped frames covered with canvas to protect their loads. From a distance on the prairie, the white canvas made the wagons look like sailing ships. They were called prairie schooners, after a type of sailing ship. The wagons carried barrels of water. Fresh water was scarce in many places on the Great Plains.

WHAT TO PACK

If you're heading west, take **EVERYTHING** you need:

★ **TOOLS:** For cooking, building, and farming.

★ **SEEDS AND ANIMALS:** To help start your new farm!

★ **HOUSEWARES:** Pots and pans, furniture, and bedding.

★ **GUNS:** Rifles and shotguns for hunting—and protection.

★ **FOOD:** Lots! Beans, cornmeal, rice, coffee, and tea. PLUS 600 pounds (270 kg) of flour, 400 pounds (180 kg) of bacon, 200 pounds (90 kg) of lard, and 100 pounds (45 kg) of sugar.

Covered wagons are ferried across the Platte River in Wyoming in this drawing made by a settler in 1859.

MANY RIVERS TO CROSS

★ **Obstacles to progress**

★ **Dangerous moments**

The wagon trails crossed many rivers on the way west. Crossing even narrow, shallow rivers was difficult for wagon trains. The oxen or horses pulling the wagons often got stuck in the mud or panicked in the cold water. It was essential to keep the wagon moving so it would not sink into the mud on the river bottom. Larger rivers were even more difficult. Settlers filled the cracks in their wagons with blankets or mud to keep out the water and float the whole thing across like a raft. The animals had to swim!

The Wagon Trails

To create trails from the Midwest to western destinations, settlers used previous routes made by Native peoples and fur trappers.

Above: Chimney Rock in Nebraska was a landmark for settlers on the Oregon Trail.

The Oregon Trail

★ **Major route to the West**

★ **Months of traveling**

The Oregon Trail was the main route for settlers heading to the West. It stretched for 2,200 miles (3,540 km), from Missouri to the Pacific Northwest. When the first wagon train set out in 1836, only part of the trail was suitable for wagons. The whole trail was later cleared. About 400,000 people made the journey.

DID YOU KNOW?

In late 1846, 87 settlers took a shortcut on the California Trail. They were trapped by snow in the mountains of the Sierra Nevada. As their food ran out, people began to die. Some survivors ate the flesh of the dead to stay alive. When they were rescued after four months, only 48 members of what was called the Donner Party survived.

THE CALIFORNIA TRAIL

★ **Heading for the goldfields**

★ **Into the deserts**

Settlers bound for California followed the Oregon Trail from Missouri. In Wyoming, however, they split off on trails that spread into the Southwest. The trail became popular after gold was discovered in California in 1848. The obstacles facing settlers on the trail included the mountains of the Sierra Nevada and the deserts of the Southwest.

The Mormon Trail

From 1846 to 1869, about 70,000 settlers used the 1,300-mile (2,090-km) Mormon Trail from Illinois to Utah. Most were Mormons seeking a place to practice their religion freely. Established Mormon settlers set up a fund to help other European Mormons pay for the trip. In the late 1850s, many of the **migrants** pushed their belongings on carts (right). They are known as the **Handcart Pioneers**.

ACROSS CANADA

★ **Fur traders blaze a trail**

★ **Using special carts**

In Canada, settlers and fur traders heading to the Northwest traveled from Fort Garry (now Winnipeg) to Fort Edmonton in what is now Alberta. Parts of the route had various names, including the Saskatchewan Trail and the Carlton Trail. The main route had been created by fur trappers who used Native trails to transport their furs east to sell. The trail was about 900 miles (1,450 km) long, with smaller routes branching off it, and took about two months to travel. Many of the travelers used "Red River carts." These were horse or ox-drawn carts with two large wheels that traveled easily over rough ground. The carts had originally been built by the Métis peoples of Canada. They were made entirely from wood, because metal to make nails was in short supply.

Above: Fort Edmonton was originally a trading post for the Hudson's Bay Company, but a town began to grow there from the 1830s.

Settling on the Plains

Most farmers on the plains were poor. They faced many challenges as they tried to grow enough food to make a living from their small plots of land.

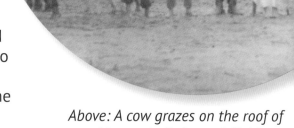

A POOR EXISTENCE

★ **Struggling to get by**

★ **Houses made from mud**

Early **homesteaders** used whatever materials they could find to build homes. There are few trees on the plains, so homesteaders built sod houses. Settlers cut squares of **turf** and stacked them to build walls. They found that the sod provided good insulation to keep homes cool in summer and warm in winter.

Above: A cow grazes on the roof of a sod house built into a hillside.

The Lure of Sheep

★ **Sheep graze the plains ...**

... and anger the cattlemen

By the late 1800s, sheep farming was growing in the West. Many of the shepherds were Mexican. Sheep were easy to raise. Most of the time, only two men were needed to look after a herd of up to 3,000 animals. Sheepmen clashed with cattle ranchers, however, in a series of "range wars." The cattlemen blamed sheep for spreading disease and overgrazing the range.

WEALTH THROUGH WHEAT

★ **Railroads own huge areas**

★ **Massive farms established**

Homesteaders weren't the only ones farming the West. The railroad companies owned large areas of land along the tracks. In places, the railroad companies used new agricultural machines to run large wheat farms of up to 100,000 acres (40,470 ha). Crews of migrant workers harvested the wheat, which was shipped east and sold for a large profit.

DID YOU KNOW?

The US Homestead Act and Canadian Dominion Lands Act each granted settlers 160 acres (65 ha) of land. To people in the East, this seemed like a lot. On the dry plains, however, the dusty soil yielded poor crops. Many settlers found that 160 acres produced barely enough corn or wheat to support a family.

Barter Economy

★ **Settlers swap goods to survive**

★ **Cash arrives later**

Instead of using money, settlers in the West often had to **barter** for goods. Sometimes they bartered or traded with Native Americans. For money they often used *wampum*—items made from tiny shell beads traditionally used in ceremonies or meetings. In mining regions, people paid for goods with the gold or silver they had dug up. As towns grew, cash became more common. The first business in any new Western town was usually a saloon. The second was often a general store, which sold everything from guns to mining tools, clothes, and food.

Right: A chief of the Ottawa nation offers wampum during trade negotiations with another nation.

Farming the Plains

Farmers in the West faced extreme conditions. The prairies were dry and open to harsh weather. Some crops grew well there, but the natural environment was often demanding.

FROM RUSSIA WITH LOVE

★ **Plant introduced by settlers**

★ **Tumbleweed spreads everywhere**

One famous plant brought to the West by settlers was tumbleweed. It gets its name because in winter, the branches form a dry ball that detaches from the roots and blows in the wind. Tumbleweed is featured in many Western movies. The plant was probably accidentally brought to the United States among seeds from Russia. It first appeared in 1880 and spread through the West.

What Grows Where

★ **Plains make growing tough**

★ **Corn is the first crop**

It could take farmers a few years to **break** the dry soil of the plains to make it suitable for farming. One of the first crops they grew there was corn. European settlers later introduced new types of wheat that were hardier and better suited to the dry environment.

European immigrants brought new types of wheat to the plains in 1874.

RAIN FOLLOWS THE PLOW

★ Theory encourages settlement ...

... but isn't actually true

A belief emerged in the 1870s that if more people farmed the plains, it would bring more rain. The belief was expressed in the saying "The rains follow the plow." The **theory** encouraged people to move to the plains, which had a dry environment. Not surprisingly, adding more settlers did not change the climate. They continued to suffer from strong winds, blizzards, and **drought**. Farmers lost their entire harvests.

The Coming of Machines

★ Large farms need large machines

★ Inventors help farmers

Below: An early tractor pulls a steel plow to turn the soil in Oregon in 1890.

The large farms that grew corn or wheat in the West were only made possible by new agricultural inventions. John Deere invented a steel plow in 1837. It was an important breakthrough. Wood or iron plows were not tough enough to turn the hard, packed soils of the prairies. Cyrus McCormick invented a mechanical **reaper** in 1831. It made it possible to harvest large areas of wheat and corn quickly. The new inventions made large-scale farming possible on the Great Plains.

Friends and Neighbors

On the Great Plains, settlers were often far from any neighbors. They had to be independent to survive, but they also needed to work together as a community.

HANGING OUT

★ **Visiting neighbors ...**

... working together

Homesteaders often lived far apart, especially on the prairies. Visits with neighbors could last three or four days. People also gathered for events such as a barn raising, where everyone helped a neighbor build a barn. When women gathered, they often worked together in a "**bee.**" They shared communal tasks such as making quilts, spinning wool, or husking corn. Bees were also a chance to share news and socialize.

School or Church?

★ **One building ...**

... several uses

In smaller settlements, everyone cooperated to construct a special building to serve the whole community. Usually the building was a schoolhouse during the week and a church on Sundays. This building was also the center of social life, offering a place for town meetings and social gatherings.

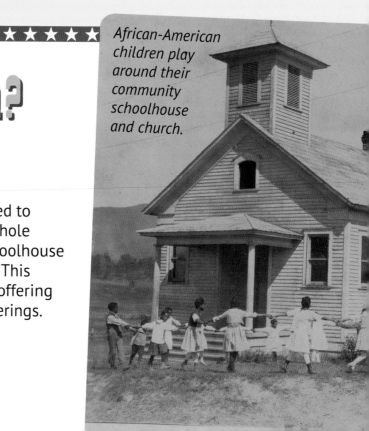

African-American children play around their community schoolhouse and church.

Ranchers and Cowboys

★ **Conflict on the range**

★ **Clashes turn to violence**

Homesteaders sometimes came into conflict with cattle ranchers. The ranchers and the cowboys who worked for them raised their cattle on the **open range**. They were angry when settlers fenced in the land they had claimed. Fencing in land became much easier after the invention of barbed wire in 1873. Ranchers and farmers also clashed over water, which was in short supply in many places.

DID YOU KNOW?

In 1873, a farmer named Joseph Glidden invented a new type of barbed wire. It was cheaper than earlier types. The wire was mass produced and easy for settlers to use.

Cowboys gather around their wagons for a meal on the range.

NO GIRLS AROUND

★ **Shortage of women**

★ **Female teachers in great demand**

Most women in the West were the wives and daughters of settlers. In mining towns and on the range, there were very few women. In fact, young men far outnumbered young women in most western places. Thousands of single young women from the East traveled west to become teachers. They usually had their pick of **suitors**, and often married when their teaching contract was done.

MY WESTERN JOURNAL

Imagine you lived in a western town. Using information on these pages, do you think life would be better for a boy or a girl? Give your reasons.

Bed and Board

Settlers ate only what they could hunt or grow. They made their own clothes and furniture. When the railroad came, it was easier to buy goods—if you had enough money.

WATER, WATER

★ **The most important resource**

★ **Often in short supply**

For all settlers, the most important concern was water. A homestead needed a reliable source of water. Some relied on rivers, creeks, or nearby lakes. In other places, settlers dug wells to get water out of underground **aquifers**. Teams of workers traveled the plains, digging wells for settlers. When water was scarce, settlers often cleaned pots and pans with sand.

Above: Farmers used windmills to pump water from deep wells.

MY WESTERN JOURNAL

The opposite page tells you about clothes in the West. If you lived on the plains, would you wear fashionable clothes? Explain reasons for your decision.

On the Move

★ **Wagons roll early**

★ **Slow progress on the plains**

Wagon trains traveled 12 to 20 miles (19 to 32 km) a day. Many settlers walked or rode their horses alongside. At night, the wagons were moved together to form a U-shape or circle. Here, the settlers made a camp. Some settlers slept in their wagons or in tents. Many others slept on the ground, wrapped in blankets.

LIVING AT HOME

Most settlers lived in a sod house (left) or a log cabin. The house had a chimney and a fireplace for cooking. The windows were filled with glass or paper waterproofed with grease to keep out the wind and rain. There was a bed, known as a "prairie rascal." If settlers had not brought furniture from the East, they made it from whatever they could find. As fuel, homesteaders burned sunflowers, hay, or dried buffalo dung known as "buffalo chips."

KEEPING UP WITH FASHION

★ **Mail-order luxuries**

★ **Style on the plains**

Godey's Lady's Book *featured these women's fashions in 1840.*

Rich settlers on the plains could read about life in the East in newspapers and magazines. They were able to order everyday items and luxuries through mail-order catalogs. Some women enjoyed magazines such as *Godey's Lady's Book*. Each issue of *Godey's* included a color illustration of a new fashion, recipes, advice, embroidery patterns, poems, short stories, and piano music. The magazine was published from 1836 to 1890. By 1860, the magazine had 150,000 readers, and was the most popular magazine in the United States.

Many Dangers

Life on the frontier was full of danger. There were wild animals, deadly diseases, and even gunfighters. For farmers, however, the biggest threat was from bad weather.

Above: A huge dust storm rolls toward a farm on the plains in Texas.

WEIRD WEATHER

★ **Dust everywhere**

★ **Twister danger**

One of the biggest dangers on the Great Plains comes from the weather. In the summer there are severe thunderstorms, and when the ground is dry the wind causes huge dust storms. In the fall, the West has more tornadoes than anywhere else in the world. And in winter, blizzards last for days and cause deep snowdrifts.

Little House on the Prairie

★ **A family affair**

★ **Facing starvation**

As a child, Laura Ingalls Wilder lived with her family in the West. Wilder later wrote children's novels based on her experiences. In her book *The Long Winter* (1940), she describes the family's struggles. The blizzards were so bad that the railroad train bringing supplies became snowbound. The family almost starved. Everyone had to spend all day twisting hay into bundles to use as fuel to keep the fire going—or they would freeze to death.

DID YOU KNOW?

Laura Ingalls Wilder's most famous book is *Little House on the Prairie*. It describes the lives of the Ingalls family in Kansas. The book also gives its name to the whole series of nine books Wilder wrote about her life. Her settler family lived in Minnesota, Iowa, South Dakota, and Missouri.

Prairie Fire!

★ **The greatest danger**

★ **A constant threat**

Fire was the biggest fear of any farmer on the prairie. The summer months were dry, and lightning could easily start a fire in the dry grass. There was no water to put it out. Settlers tried to stop a fire by lighting smaller fires to burn the ground around it. That way, there was nothing for the larger fire to burn. Digging fire breaks had the same effect. Farmers cleared strips of open earth between patches of crops so a fire had nothing to burn, and could not spread.

BIBLICAL PLAGUE

★ **Insects stop trains**

★ **Farmers ruined**

Huge **infestations** of grasshoppers could destroy crops and buildings. They could even eat the clothes off your back if you were caught in a swarm. The worst plague came in 1874 when grasshoppers spread across the entire Great Plains. The insects covered the railroad tracks, slowing down or stopping the trains. Many farming families lost their crops. They were forced to return to the East.

ARMED CLASHES

★ **Wars on the range**

★ **Settlers vs ranchers**

In the early days of the West, violence sometimes broke out between ranchers and settlers. These conflicts were known as range wars. Both sides hired gunfighters to help them. The outlaw Billy the Kid came to fame fighting in the 1878 Lincoln County War between ranchers in New Mexico. The Johnson County War in Wyoming lasted from 1889 to 1893. Many settlers were killed by ranchers who wanted to keep them off the open range.

Left: Billy the Kid is believed to have killed eight men—but the total may be as high as 21.

Take It Easy

In the evenings, families would gather to play music, read aloud, or play cards. Many settlers were Christian, and going to church on Sunday was a social event.

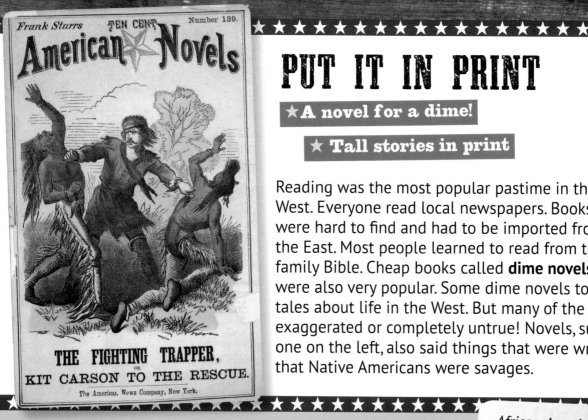

Frank Starrs TEN CENT. Number 139.
American Novels
THE FIGHTING TRAPPER,
OR.
KIT CARSON TO THE RESCUE.
The American News Company, New York.

PUT IT IN PRINT

★ **A novel for a dime!**

★ **Tall stories in print**

Reading was the most popular pastime in the West. Everyone read local newspapers. Books were hard to find and had to be imported from the East. Most people learned to read from their family Bible. Cheap books called **dime novels** (left) were also very popular. Some dime novels told exciting tales about life in the West. But many of the stories were exaggerated or completely untrue! Novels, such as the one on the left, also said things that were wrong, such as that Native Americans were savages.

Building a Community

★ **Former slaves settle a town**

★ **Church is social center**

African Americans from the South settled Nicodemus, Kansas, in 1877. The town struggled to survive before more black settlers arrived in 1878 and 1879 with better farm equipment. By 1800, Nicodemus had a population of 400. The citizens built a stone church in 1885. The church was the center of social events, such as the annual celebration of the emancipation of the slaves in 1863.

African-American settlers in Nicodemus, Kansas, stand in front of the town's first stone church.

CHAUTAUQUA

★ **Community summer camps**

★ **Assemblies throughout the West**

In the late 1800s, many settlers attended Chautauqua Assemblies. These were outdoor gatherings held in tents over two or three days. The whole community came to hear talks by popular speakers, and to see musicians and entertainers. The gatherings aimed to provide stimulating and uplifting entertainment for rural Americans. The assemblies toured small towns throughout the West. They took their name from Chautauqua Lake in Illinois, where the first one took place in 1874. The assemblies were popular until the 1920s. President Theodore Roosevelt was said to have called them "the most American thing in America."

Left: This Chautauqua Assembly was held in Indiana in 1908.

Pulpit Superstars

★ **Traveling preachers**

★ **Camp revivals**

Among the superstars in the West were traveling preachers. Preachers set up a camp and gave dramatic sermons. These **camp meetings** were popular because many settlers had no regular church to attend. Even those who could attend church went to camp meetings or "revivals" to see famous preachers such as Billy Sunday, a former baseball player. These meetings became social events where people could see friends and enjoy a picnic.

DID YOU KNOW?

Settlers in the West were some of the first Americans to cycle for leisure. The first modern bicycles appeared in North America around 1890. They were soon sold in the West. Settlers cycled long distances and explored the natural landscape around them.

Native Americans

The arrival of settlers and farmers on the Great Plains had a terrible impact on the Native peoples who already lived there.

This photograph shows a family of Sioux.

THE PLAINS PEOPLES

★ **Native peoples of the plains**

★ **Different ways of life**

Settlers on the plains claimed land that was already home to Native peoples. Some of the Plains nations were **nomads**. They moved around the plains to hunt buffalo. They included the Blackfoot, Cheyenne, Comanche, Lakota, and some Apache, Cree, and Shoshone peoples. Other plains peoples lived in semi-permanent villages. The Iowa, Mandan, Omaha, Osage, and Wichita peoples grew crops such as corn and squash.

Following the Bison

★ **Hunting the buffalo**

★ **Open range under threat**

The Plains peoples were expert hunters. They used horses to hunt buffalo (bison) with bows and arrows (left), or herded them over cliffs. The buffalo provided meat, and the skin was used to make clothes and shelter. As settlers fenced in the open land and built towns and railroads, it became difficult for Native peoples to follow herds of buffalo across the plains.

CONFLICT

★ **Wars with the government**

★ **Victories and defeats**

Some of the best land on the plains belonged to Native peoples. The US and Canadian governments wanted to force the Plains peoples onto **reservations**, so that settlers could move onto their land. Some nations fought back. In 1876, the Great Sioux War broke out between the Lakota and their allies and the US Army. In February 1877, the Sioux were defeated and forced onto a reservation. In Canada, Métis settlers and Native allies also resisted land claims made by the government, but their efforts were crushed in the Northwest Rebellion of 1885.

Above: The Lakota Sioux won a famous victory over US General George Custer in the Battle of the Little Bighorn on June 25, 1876.

End of Resistance

★ **Ghost Dance movement**

★ **Last hope fails**

In 1890, Wovoka, a **seer** from the Paiute peoples, claimed Native peoples could take their lands back from white Americans by dancing ritual dances. This Ghost Dance movement spread quickly through the peoples of the plains. It reached as far as California. Ultimately, the movement failed. In December 1890, 128 Sioux and 31 US soldiers died in the Battle of Wounded Knee in South Dakota. The clash at Wounded Knee marked the last armed resistance by the Plains peoples.

MY WESTERN JOURNAL

Imagine you lived among the Plains peoples. Would you be prepared to fight to keep white settlers off your tribal lands? Give your reasons.

DID YOU KNOW?

In 1887, the Dawes Act split Native American reservation land into lots for families. Since the lots were only up to 160 acres (65 sq km), there was often tribal land left over. The US government seized this land and gave it to white settlers.

The Legacy of Settlement

The US Census Office declared the Frontier closed in 1890. The American West had been settled. In Canada, the largest wave of immigration to the West was about to begin.

Omaha, Nebraska, became a successful town thanks to its transportation links.

SETTLING THE PLAINS

★ **Centers on the prairies**

★ **Towns with ambitions**

The plains still reflect the pattern of early settlement. Many early settlers founded towns. They had great ambitions that they could attract enough settlers to thrive. Many built large city halls and churches in the hope of growing far bigger. Many towns failed to grow, however, perhaps because no railroad was built near them. Today, some plains towns still have low populations—but huge city halls.

On the Reservations

★ **Living on poor land**

★ **Keeping old ways alive**

By the 1890s, most Native Americans lived on reservations. Reservations were often on poor land that no white settlers wanted to farm. Western settlement hurt the Native peoples' ways of life by removing them from their homes. Today, many nations across North America are trying to reclaim rights to their land. They also take part in traditional customs (left) to keep their cultures alive.

Statehood Spreads

★ **Entering the Union**

★ **End of the Frontier**

When settlers first arrived on the Great Plains, the region was divided into territories of the United States. As the population grew, settlers wanted to form states. If a territory became a state, the federal government became responsible for providing better services, such as law enforcement, mail services, and transportation links. Kansas became a state in 1861, Nebraska in 1867, Colorado in 1876, the Dakotas and Montana in 1889, and Wyoming in 1890. Oklahoma, which had previously been known as Indian Territory, became a state in 1907.

MODERN FARMING

★ **America's breadbasket**

★ **Machines on the plains**

Huge farms on the Great Plains still provide most of America's wheat. There are nearly 125,000 square miles (323,750 sq km) of wheat farming. Most of the wheat is based on the varieties introduced to Kansas by Mennonite farmers from Russia in 1874. Nearly 40 percent of the wheat crop is **exported**. Canada is the sixth-largest producer of wheat in the world and exports 60 percent of its crop.

Right: Combine harvesters cut wheat on the Great Plains.

GLOSSARY

aquifers Underground layers of rock that contain water

barter To exchange goods or services for other goods or services

bee A meeting to complete a communal task

break To prepare land for crops by plowing it

camp meetings Religious meetings held in tents or in the open air

Conestoga wagons Large covered wagons used to travel long distances

dime novels Cheap paperback novels that told dramatic and sensational stories

drought A long period of low rainfall

emancipation Setting someone free from slavery

exported Sold to someone in another country

Handcart Pioneers Settlers who pushed and pulled small wheeled carts by hand overland to carry goods

harrassment Repeatedly bothering or picking on someone

homesteaders Settlers who claim federal land

immigrants People who move permanently to a new country or region

infestation An overwhelming number of insects

migrants People who move from one place to another to try to find a better way of life

nomads People with no fixed home who instead move from place to place

open range Large areas of unfenced public land

prairies Large areas of open grassland

prejudice Ideas and judgments made about a person or race before knowing them

reaper A machine that cuts standing crops

reservations Areas set aside for use by Native Americans

seer A person who sees supernatural visions of the future

stake a claim To claim a piece of ground by marking its boundaries with stakes

suitors Single men who are looking for wives

theory A possible explanation for a belief

treaty An agreement between two groups of people or nations

turf The surface of the ground, where grass grows

uninhabitable Unsuitable for living

William Becknall opens the Santa Fe Trail from Franklin, Missouri, to Santa Fe, which is then in Mexican territory.

March 2: Texas declares independence from Mexico. After a war, Texans create the Republic of Texas.

May 22: Up to 1,000 migrants set out on the Oregon Trail in what becomes known as the Great Migration.

July 24: The first Mormons reach the Great Salt Lake in Utah Territory, after traveling along the Mormon Trail.

1821 1836   1840   1843   1847   1848

May 25: A small party of settlers sets out from Independence, Missouri, along what will become the Oregon Trail.

Three wagons become the first wagon train to travel the length of the Oregon Trail.

February 18: The survivors of the Donner Party are rescued after becoming stranded on the California Trail and forced to eat dead bodies to stay alive.

January 24: Gold is discovered at Sutter's Mill in California, starting a Gold Rush.

ON THE WEB

http://www.nps.gov/oreg/learn/historyculture/index.htm
A page from the National Parks Service about the Oregon Trail.

http://www.history.com/topics/donner-party
A page from History.com about the Donner Party.

http://www.historybits.com/west-wagon-trains.htm
A History Bits page about the covered wagons on the wagon trails.

http://www.fasttrackteaching.com/burns/Unit_2_Westward/U2_adaptations_inventions_plains.html
A page about how new inventions helped settlement on the Great Plains

https://history.lds.org/section/pioneer-story?lang=eng
Pages about the Mormon Trail from the Church of Jesus Christ of the Latter-Day Saints.

BOOKS

Landau, Elaine. *The Oregon Trail* (True Books: American History). Children's Press, 2006.

Morley, Jacqueline. *You Wouldn't Want to Be an American Pioneer*. Franklin Watts, 2012.

Rajczak, Kristen. *Life on a Wagon Train* (What You Didn't Know About History). Gareth Stevens Publishing, 2013.

Steele, Christy. *Famous Wagon Trails* (America's Westward Expansion). World Almanac Library, 2005.

February 2: At the end of the Mexican–American War, California and the Southwest become part of the United States.

May 10: The first transatlantic railroad line is completed, ending the age of the wagon trains.

July: A grasshopper plague devastates crops across much of the Great Plains.

Lakota Native Americans and their allies fight the US Army in the Great Sioux War. They are forced to surrender the following year.

1862   **1869**   **1874**   **1876**   **1890**

May 20: The Homesteader Act makes it easy for settlers to claim up to 160 acres (65 ha) of public land in the West.

Mennonite settlers introduce to Kansas new types of wheat that grow particularly well on the Great Plains.

The US Census Bureau announces that the Frontier is now closed. All of the United States is now settled.

INDEX

A

African Americans 6, 24

B

barbed wire 19
Billy the Kid 23
boosters 29
buffalo 26
buffalo chips 21

C

California Gold Rush 6, 7, 12
California Trail 8, 12
Canada 4, 5, 6, 13, 27, 29
cattle ranchers 14, 19, 23
Chautauqua Assemblies 25
clothing 21
Conestoga wagons 10
cowboys 6, 19
Custer, General George A. 27

D

Dawes Act 27
Deere, John 17
Dominion Lands Act 5, 15
Donner Party 12

F

farms 16, 17, 20, 29
food 11
fur trappers 13

G

Ghost Dance 27
Godey's Lady's Book 21
grasshoppers 23
Great Plains 5, 10, 14–15,
    16–17, 22, 23, 26–27, 28–29
Great Sioux War 27

H

Handcart Pioneers 13
homes and housing 14, 21
Homestead Act 5, 15

IJK

immigrants 7, 29
Independence, Missouri 9, 10
Johnson County War 23
Kansas 6, 24, 29

L

Lakota peoples 26, 27
Little Bighorn, Battle of the 27
Little House on the Prairie 22
Louisiana Territory 4, 5

M

map 8–9
McCormick, Cyrus 17
Mennonites 5, 29
Métis peoples 13, 27
Mormon Trail 7, 13
Mormons 5, 7, 8
My Western Journal 5, 6, 19, 20,
    27

N

Native peoples 4, 12, 15, 26–27
Nicodemus, Kansas 24
Northwest Rebellion 27

OP

Oregon Trail 8, 9, 12
pastimes 24–25
Plains peoples 26

R

railroads 7, 15, 29
range wars 14, 23
Red River carts 13
religion 5, 13, 25
reservations 27, 28

S

Salt Lake City 8
Santa Fe Railroad 29
Santa Fe Trail 8
Saskatchewan Trail 8, 13
Schmidt, C. B. 29
settlers 5, 12–13, 14–15, 16,
    18–19, 23
sheep farming 14
Sioux peoples 27
slaves 6, 24
sod houses 14, 21
statehood 29
Sunday, Billy 25

TU

teachers 19
tumbleweed 16
Utah 7, 8

W

wagon trails 8–9, 11, 12–13
wagon trains 6, 10–11, 12, 20
wampum 15
weather 17, 22
wells 20
wheat 15, 16, 17, 29
Wilder, Laura Ingalls 22
women 18, 19, 21
Wounded Knee, Battle of 27
Wovoka 27

Y

Young, Brigham 7, 8

32